"An engaging, actionable, and provocative book about phone calls to parents? I was skeptical at first, but then I read it. When you combine Mike Goldstein's cut-to-the-chase smarts with Match's proven learning about what actually works, you get a potent, witty, and behavior-changing exploration of one of a teacher's most important tools for accelerating student learning."

Steven Farr, Chief Knowledge Officer,
Teach for America

"Too many books about teachers, students and families just focus on bake sales, behavior challenges, or missing backpacks. While those things have a time and place, this book highlights the why, what, and how for teachers building strong and productive relationships with families. It is full of practical training advice, clear rationale for family outreach, and simply no excuse for not making it happen. As someone who obsesses about teacher time, I was impressed how the book spells out how long outreach will take and why it is worth it. If only this book had existed when I was teaching!"

Maia Heyck-Merlin, author of *The Together Teacher* and founder
of The Together Group, former Chief Talent Officer of Achievement First

"I've been teaching a number of Match Education's practices and procedures to my pre-service teachers for several years now—including phone calls with parents—to great effect. I'm thrilled that *Phoning Parents* (which I'll be assigning!) codifies Match's insightful, straightforward, and good-humored approach to a crucial tool for building powerful, productive relationships with students and their parents."

Scott Seider, Assistant Professor of Education,
Boston University

D1506899

"Such a quick and impactful read, from some of the most successful urban educators. Teach For America staff and teachers have raved for years about these ideas."

Wendy Kopp, Founder & Chair
of Teach For America

"*Phoning Parents* is a wonderful book that teaches teachers how to open their hearts and classrooms to parents. When parents can become co-architects in their children's learning, magic happens! A must read for every educator!"

Terry Grier, Superintendent of Houston Unified School District

"*Phoning Parents* is engagingly written and totally and pragmatically useful to any teacher or administrator. It'll not only make you better at the phone calls you make now but help you see new opportunities to use communication with parents to help students succeed."

Doug Lemov, Managing Director,
Uncommon Schools, Taxonomy Project

"Children benefit when there is good communication between home and school, and respect between families and teachers. Although widely acknowledged, these important connections often don't happen. *Phoning Parents* provides specific ways for teachers use phone calls skillfully to build these bridges: when to call, ways to say specific things, how to consider particular situations or challenges. With its clear focus on practice, it can help beginning teachers get started and support more experienced teachers refine their use of phone calls home."

Deborah Loewenberg Ball,
University of Michigan School of Education and TeachingWorks

Phoning Parents

High-leverage
moves to transform
your classroom &
restore your sanity

Michael Goldstein

Kids don't care
how much you know
until they know
how much you care.

—Charles Sposato

Table of Contents

Chapter One

My name is Mike Goldstein. I learned
a teaching secret from a guy named
Charlie Sposato. He learned it
from somebody else.

Charlie taught middle and high school English for 33 years in the Boston area. He often was able to motivate some very tough kids who didn't connect with other teachers. He'd get them to try hard.

He was honored as Massachusetts Teacher of the Year in 1990. Years later, when I was courting him to become the founding principal of a new school in Boston, I did some "reference checks" beyond the normal talking to his colleagues (who raved about him). I also approached some of the tougher-looking kids smoking cigarettes in the Framingham High School parking lot. I asked if they knew Mr. Sposato. After deciding not to rough me up, a few guys took turns telling stories about how his was the only class where they'd show up and try hard.

Charlie flourished with the less tough kids, too. With some students, he instilled a lifelong love of literature and poetry. He would leverage his enormous knowledge of the classics to connect kids with books and ideas they'd like. With the other kids, even if he wasn't a "life-changing teacher" from their perspective and "merely" a very good one, he got them to learn lots of nuts and bolts English — to read critically, to interpret, to write, to analyze, and so forth.

Charlie was almost chosen as NASA's teacher-in-space on the Space Shuttle Challenger in 1986. But it was his friend Christa McAuliffe instead who flew on the doomed mission. Mostly he lived the relatively anonymous life of the hyper-skilled public school teacher.

I met him in 2000. I had just graduated with a master's degree from Harvard in education policy. I was a bit on the smug side, I'll admit it. At age 28, I'd been given the green light to open my own charter school -- Match. I was filled with harebrained ideas. But I did have a few gems, and one was to hire this guy as our founding principal. He was the real deal.

I still remember the first day of school. Charlie had greeted all the kids at the door: a short Italian guy shaking hands with black and Hispanic boys and girls, teaching them his greeting ritual, insisting that they look him in the eye, have a firm grip, have a conversation. Now, with all the kids settled into period one classes, Charlie was dialing parents. It was around 8:45 am. He'd phone one after another, parent after parent. Just short conversations, to check in, say hello.

This went on for over an hour. It was clear that even though it was the first day of school in September, Charlie had already called many parents multiple times during August. I asked him what he was doing. We'd never covered "phone calls to parents" as a topic in education classes I'd taken at Harvard. "Doing what I've always done," he said. "Building relationships with parents by calling them on the phone."

He taught this technique to every Match teacher. Did it work? Yes.

Now how can I get you to believe that? Dearest Reader, some of you are "logical thinkers" and some of you are "emotional thinkers." Let me address you in turn.

To the first group, let me mention: under Charlie's leadership, Match went on to become one of the highest performing charter schools in the nation, working with a student population that was 20% special needs, 75% low-income, and 90% black and Hispanic. This was measured by test scores and college success rates; the think tank Mathematica named Match High School as the top charter school in the nation for several years from 2008 to 2012 (Google "EPIC Mathematica" to learn more).

Does our school have any flaws? Many. Does our team feel we must improve dramatically? YES. But several hundred Boston families apply each year for a few dozen slots. That's in part because parents have heard that our educators are accessible and caring, and that sort of reputation comes from the proactive phone calls.

To the second group of readers, the more emotional thinkers, consider this: when Charlie died of cancer in 2007, the church was jam-packed with his former students. Hundreds. It was a ceremony filled with tears and joy. (Google "Charlie Sposato obituary" if you want to know more). Kids knew he cared. One way he showed them he cared was to respect their parents.

Charlie was a successful educator for many reasons. But none was greater, in his mind, than his ability and willingness to build relationships with the parents of his students. Most teachers do care about their students. I'm sure you do.

But Charlie's strength was his ability to **communicate** that he cared — particularly to parents who might be skeptical of that fact, as they'd been "burned" before, and tended not to trust teachers and principals. Charlie could build authentic relationships with even the wariest students, in part by enlisting their parents.

This fundamental strength of Charlie's has served as a guiding principle for the Match Schools, a tutoring program that has been implemented across the nation, and our own graduate school of education. Charlie's genius in building relationships profoundly influenced me and the rest of the team at Match.

Neither parents nor kids necessarily expect teacher phone calls, so the act itself — whatever the words exchanged — helps convey you want to go above and beyond. A call works the same way it does when you call your spouse or significant other just to say hello: it says, "I am thinking about you." This book is about how — if you can suspend a dozen or more legitimate concerns you will have — you can, like Charlie, and like thousands of other teachers, systematically build relationships with parents that allow you to:

1 Hold kids to a much higher behavioral expectation.

2 Get kids to work much harder in class and at home.

3 Hold the line with your academic standards, even when kids sometimes fail to reach them.

4 Emotionally feel better as a teacher while doing all of these things, because you feel a sense of common purpose with the parent.

I know. It sounds gooey and idealistic. But this strategy isn't just some cross-stitched slogan you pin to your wall. A routine of making short, proactive phone calls can be a high-leverage strategy for getting kids to do the work you've assigned, to try hard, and behave well in your class. Spending 30 minutes a night calling parents will, we believe, generate far more student motivation than you tinkering with your lesson plans for 30 minutes a night.

Technical note: From here on out, when we say "parent," we mean that to include guardian or other adult (Grandma, Uncle Fred, foster parent) who is the key adult in a kid's life. We sometimes say she, sometimes he (although she is more common in our world). There, done with technical note.

You won't learn about parent phone calls in graduate school. It's one of those "secrets of the profession."

So how much do phone calls help?

To measure it, we actually hired two Harvard economists to run a randomized trial. Now granted, these guys were Harvard doctoral students at the time. So they were fairly cheap. But still smart.

We did a careful experiment. The set-up was simple. Some parents in summer school got teacher phone calls each night. Other parents (picked at random) did not. The research question: What happened the next day in class?

The results were powerful.

- **Teacher-parent communication increased the odds a student completed their homework by 42%.**

- **Teacher-parent communication reduced the amount of time spent redirecting students by 25%.**

- **Teacher-parent communication increased students raising their hands by 49%.**

Was this a perfect study? No. Was it a serious work of research? Yes, and published by a major journal. Will those results be what you experience? Who knows? Your reality will almost certainly be somewhat better or worse. Is this study the first-ever research that has ever been conducted on the effect of teacher phone calls to parents? Yes.

If you want to read the study, Google "The Effect of Teacher-Family Communication on Student Engagement: Evidence from a Randomized Field Experiment." So why did phone calls to parents help the teacher so much? Matt and Shaun write:

We identify three primary mechanisms through which communication likely affected engagement: stronger teacher-student relationships, expanded parental involvement, and increased student motivation.

How do phone calls to parents work? What's the big picture?

From a student's point of view, your class is like spinach.

Some kids like spinach. So they'll gladly eat it. They'll show up and enjoy your class. Yum, math class.

Other kids know that spinach is good for them, nutritious. They want to feel healthy. So they'll eat spinach, sometimes a bit grudgingly, so long as there is a little encouragement from you, and/or garlic salt.

But a certain percentage of kids just hate spinach. They don't understand why they should have to eat it. They arrive to your class not wanting to be there. Nothing personal. They just would not show up if they were not required to. We call these reluctant learners.

That's where you come in, teacher.

One way you can get a reluctant learner to eat some spinach is as a favor of sorts to you. And why do you a favor? Because you actually believe the kid can succeed. You expect the very best of him. You legitimately see him as someone with great potential and on the path to college. When he picks up that vibe, if it's authentic, it makes him want to eat the spinach, at least some of it, at least for a while. If his peers try hard, too, there will be a multiplier effect.

Metaphor Alert for The Haters.

For those of you who get worked up about analogies, we are betting big cash right now that you hate our comparing spinach to your class. You prefer that your class be compared to: Symphony! Sonnet! Journey!

(your class)

Yep. Hate on us all you want, but the reality is some of your students probably don't see it that way. Remember, we're giving you their perception. Not ours. Okay, end Metaphor Alert.

Relationships with parents help you improve the learning of all students: the spinach lovers, the spinach begrudgers, and the spinach haters.

In particular, the most plausible way a spinach begrudger will work hard in your class is: if you have a personal relationship with her as an individual, one that is grounded in the notion that you are a demanding teacher who absolutely must have her attention, her effort, and her learning and that the reason you have these expectations is you genuinely believe in her potential, and care about her success.

Typically spinach-begrudging students have had disappointing experiences with school. They might not care about any big learning goals yet. They might not have a long-term time horizon. They might lack grit.

A skilled teacher often overcomes this because the kids know she authentically cares about them as individuals. They don't want to let her down.

Now it gets tricky. Other teachers may have professed these sentiments to these exact same students. May have said "I care." But then the teacher's actions belied this message.

For example, think about the Very Nice Teacher who asks a student a lot about his life and his interests, about sports and video games, and church and friends, and their plans for the coming weekend. Going for: "I care." But the VNT lets that same kid get away with stuff, both behaviorally and academically, during class.

This makes students wary. They've heard "I care" before. And sometimes not just from teachers. Sometimes from family who talk a big game but don't back it up with action.

The Very Nice Teacher does have a relationship with the student. But what message is sent? Kid wonders: "Does that teacher really expect my best? If so, why am I so obviously able to get away with less than my best?"

Imagine if your students were asked:

"What teacher (current or past) pushes you to do your very best?"

Would they name you?

That's a key word: push. Sometimes your topic, or your reading, or your lesson, or your problem set will be so interesting and provocative that you'll inspire kids to do their best — just from the sheer attraction of the ideas in play. That is wonderful.

But you can't bank on that. You probably can't deliver that sort of lesson each day. If you can, please return this book for a full refund, and enclose an autographed photo for us, so we can worship you.

You can always, however, earn a reputation from parents and kids alike as a straightforward teacher who really believes each student can work hard and therefore succeed: a never-ending conveyor of the "Effort = Success" message.

If you invest out-of-class time advancing the message of high expectations, by specifically praising hard work and good choices, and by really nailing the little things when they happen, you'll be one of the positive teachers that kids name.

However, if you invest out-of-class time with each student just getting to know them, asking about their lives, without pushing your message of

high academic expectations — then they'd rate you very high on "nice" and "cares" — but low on "demands excellence from me in the classroom and in my homework and studying."

So, again, we're talking about a very particular type of relationship-building.

If you can physically look up and down the aisles of your class with a sense of...

Wow, I have really connected with each of these kids; they will really give me latitude to push them: on assignments, on tests, on questions, on behavior. I'm not stressed because even when I demand excellence, they know I care, and their parents have my back.

...then you are in a good position to confidently teach, even to those children who — until you change their minds — think of your class as "spinach."

What does research say?

There is great empirical evidence of these three things:

1 Student engagement during class leads to more learning (duh).

2 Student engagement can be raised with perception that teachers care.

3 Involving parents can increase student achievement.

Here's the wonky version of those three sentences: Existing research has documented that students' engagement in school is continuously shaped by their relationships with adults and their schooling environment (Connell, 1990; Finn & Rock, 1997).

A large body of evidence also documents the important role teachers play in molding student engagement (Battistich, Solomon, Watson, & Schaps, 1997; Furrer & Skinner, 2003; Ryan & Patrick, 2001). Specifically, demonstrated teacher caring has been shown to be associated with increases in students' academic effort (Wentzel, 1997, 1998), which is suggestive of how emotional engagement might translate into cognitive engagement.

Parents also play a central role in shaping their children's behavior and engagement in school. Earlier work has shown that

involving parents in their children's schooling can improve students' academic achievement (Barnard, 2004; Seitsinger et al., 2008).

Whew, did your eyes just glaze over? Ours did too.

The real question is how can a teacher — particularly an individual teacher like you — involve parents?

Sure, you can open your classroom to parents, and be invitational. We think that is a great idea. And that approach is not the norm, argue some leading education writers. Jay Matthews of *The Washington Post* has written that parents are often made to feel unwelcome in schools.

In Virginia, one guy actually tried to create a law to make schools be more open to parent visits.

A member of Virginia's House of Delegates made a classroom visit, saw his daughter learn to read, and loved it.

Jay Matthews writes:

So when he saw my columns about school districts discouraging such observations, he decided to do something. He added this sentence to his House Bill No. 400 on education:

'Local school boards shall adopt and implement policies to ensure that the parent or legal guardian of a student or prospective student enrolled in the school division may, subject to reasonable notice and with minimized disruption,

act as an observer in the child's classroom.'

I don't expect (his) bill to get far.

Luckily as a teacher, you don't have to make law or set school policy to connect with parents. You can set class policy (typically). Should you invite parents in?

But isn't that scary, parents visiting your class?

Andy Rotherham of *Time Magazine* quotes a teacher, Brittany Clark: *I feel that if I am doing my job, then I have nothing to fear upon the arrival of a parent or any visitor, for that matter. As a public servant and a member of a profession that has recently come under fire, the best thing we as teachers can do is to have an open-door policy that shows our nation that good teachers have nothing to hide.*

So let's agree that it's helpful for parents to visit your classroom.

Here's the catch. This is very hard to arrange. If you teach in a high-poverty school and roll out the welcome mat, most parents **won't** take you up on it.

The same thing is true when you give out your phone number to parents. Few parents call you. Particularly parents of the kids who "need the most help."

Other parent involvement techniques — sending emails, letters, newsletters, or report cards filled with comments — are also nice ideas. However, they are limited. First, there's no dialogue. No way for the parent to easily communicate back to you. And therefore there's very little ability to come up with practical solutions together. Email is also a difficult way to have a charged conversation. Email eliminates vocal tone and nonverbal cues which are essential.

Arne Duncan, the Secretary of Education, has said: "The best way for parents to learn about the quality of public schools is by observing teachers in the classroom and seeing how the principal leads the school."

Carol Peck, former National Superintendant of the Year, has said: "Wise principals and teachers encourage parents to visit, observe and ask questions."

Six Reasons

There are six reasons we believe proactive phone calls are the ***best*** parent engagement strategy.

1 A phone call shows courtesy and respect, which both the parent and the student notice.

Student: "When she spoke to my mom, it was like building a bond with the school, making me feel like the classroom was my second home, like she was like a sister to me."

2 You're more confident because you know the parent received and absorbed the information, rather than just sending home documents and hoping for the best.

Teacher: "After I've made a bunch of parent calls, I find I can ask more of [students] in class without risk of backlash, and they're more willing to allow me to push them/ talk them down. These calls make my instructions seems less like a dictatorship and more like reasonable requests."

3 Phone calls convey information to parents better than other methods.

Parental involvement in their children's academics is often limited by the information asymmetry that exists between students and their parents, especially with students in secondary school who see five or more teachers in a day. At a basic level, phone calls home provide parents with more detailed information about their child's academic progress and behavior that has not been filtered by students.

4 Phone calls are the best method to allow teachers to gain information ***from parents.***

These include contextual information on what a kid may be going through at home, and strategies for addressing behavior that are successful at home.

5 Phone calls allow a teacher to provide specific advice if the parent is open to it.

Teacher: "Earl's reading quiz scores were steadily decreasing. I spoke with his mom a couple of times about the necessity of reading really carefully during the evenings. She asked what she might try. I suggested that some other parents got kids to turn off the phone and TV. His grades went up significantly."

6 Phone calls to parents can get kids to take you up on your offer to talk to them on the phone.

"When I call parents, my students definitely showed more interest and investment in their learning. For instance, some would call or text for clarifying [homework] problems etc."

Why We Believe You Should Call All Your Parents (rather than the "strugglers" only)

We've observed that teachers tend to loosely divide students into six categories. Certainly kids (just like parents) are far more complex than six categories could possibly encapsulate. Still, we think it's helpful to group traits together. We also named each combo for maximum recall effect.

Category	Grades	Behavior	Effort	Percent of Total Kids
Kinzena Rock Your Socks Off	Solid	Good	High	45%
Susie Solid Slacker	Solid	Good	Low	15%
Tom Troubled	Solid	Bad	Low	5%
Unskilled Ulysses	Low	Good	High	5%
Shrugging Sarah	Low	Good	Low	20%
Driving Me Crazy David	Low	Bad	Low	10%

You will undoubtedly think of other, legitimate, ways to classify students. But in any case, we believe this is how many kids view themselves.

Many teachers tend to invest most of their phone calls to just 15% of the kids: **Tom Troubled** and **Driving Me Crazy David.** Kids in the other four categories tend to get far, far less teacher communication.

This situation is problematic. The other 25% of kids who are at-risk for failing (**Unskilled Ulysses** and **Shrugging Sarah**) need your support, and their parents need to be informed of their progress.

Susie Solid Slacker (another 15% of your kids) may not be failing at the moment, but lack of effort is going to hurt her down the road. Maybe by high school, for sure by college. If you can "flip" her this year into being more responsible, you'll be helping her forever more.

Kinzena Rock Your Socks Off is doing fine, but is she doing great? She'd benefit from positive reinforcement and occasional help, reminders, and corrections. What if her dream is to be a doctor? To do that, she'll almost certainly have to be incredible in school, an A+ student in your high-poverty school, so she can ultimately compete against A students from suburban and prep schools where the average level of academic difficulty is much higher. If you let Kinzena keep plugging along with an A- in your classroom, aren't you making it fairly unlikely she'll achieve her dream?

Just like Charlie Sposato showed us before Match even opened its doors, proactive phone calls are tremendously powerful investments.

TEN REASONS NOT TO CALL PARENTS

Chapter Two

We list these because
we believe if you recognize the issues,
you can overcome them.

1

Fear of Conflict

This is natural. If you call a parent to explain that his little darling is not trying hard or is distracting other kids, you might get an earful of complaints, rationalization, and blame. Hence your aversion to phone calls.

And we agree: If the first time you call home is with a problem, then you're more likely to get an unhappy and uncooperative parent. They might even yell at you or blame you. We're not fans of the "Just call home when there is a problem" approach to parent communication.

However, if you combine the techniques we describe in Chapter 4 (noticing good things that each student does, then making many proactive Praise Calls to build up relationship capital), you can then "spend down" that relationship capital with Correction Calls.

The other tradeoff to consider: if you overcome your fear of conflict with parents (who might challenge your version of things), it might help to lessen your fear of conflict with students.

Teachers say when they've made parent phone calls, they have lower fear of conflict during class — because the parent "has their back."

2

Belief That Your Parents Are Unusually Difficult To Deal With

---

Are the parents of your students tougher, rougher, and less caring than those of other teachers? If so, calling wouldn't accomplish much, because "your" parents Do Not Care.

Our guess is that while sometimes it feels that way, it's unlikely that your students are the "toughest" around. We've surveyed teachers in every type of inner-city school, and keep coming to the same conclusion: the vast majority of parents of children in high-poverty schools are, like any other parents, good people who deeply care about their kids. They want their kids to do well in school.

This is probably true of the parents of your students, too. If you assume the best in them, and call frequently, you will often be rewarded with cooperation, appreciation, and visible change in their children. Not *always* rewarded — that is too high a bar — but often.

There will always be outlier parents who ARE difficult. They make calling a little unpleasant. That is true of any demographic in any locality in the world. These outliers are outnumbered and outweighed by the majority of parents who appreciate teachers a great deal and want to help them educate their children. If you put faith in this belief and try more parent communication, we believe you'll come to the same conclusions pretty quickly.

3

It's Not The Job of A Teacher To Call Parents

That's a value judgment. Again, we get it. It would be nice if we lived in a world where teachers didn't need to call parents. We wish that kids went to bed at a reasonable time; had notebooks and pencils; had done the homework or at least made a good effort; had breakfast; had a lifetime of access to books, conversations with rich vocabulary, museums; and overall were in a good position to focus during class.

That world certainly does exist in many suburban school classrooms, and in many prep schools. In those places, a teacher can "focus on teaching." (That is, the tasks we traditionally associate with teaching).

But that's not typically how things work in high-poverty schools. For a variety of reasons, many of the students at these schools don't always arrive to your class ready to learn.

So you have a choice:

A. Teach the willing students, those ready to learn...(while always being professional and encouraging to the other children, but realizing their limits).

B. Invest hours every week into "flipping" the at-first unwilling children into willing learners; if you want to do that, then you do need to call parents as a high-leverage strategy.

4

The Overly Chatty Parent

Sometimes teachers call up a parent, but then can't get off the phone. This isn't the majority of calls for sure, but when it happens, it's almost debilitating. You keep waiting for the right moment to exit, but the parent seems to go into monologue mode for several minutes at a time. Heck, we have several relatives who fit this description.

Sometimes this manifests in a negative way — complaining about the school, for example. Other times it's perfectly pleasant — amiable conversation about the parent's job or the goings-on with the child — but it just takes so long that you feel reluctant to call the parent again. You fear another lost 20 minutes when you really need to get a lesson plan done.

Chapter 4 suggests techniques for how to avoid this, mostly by being very specific up-front about how long the call will be.

5

You're Too Busy

These phone calls take time. Valuable time. Teachers are busy. Very busy.

You could be otherwise be lesson planning or sleeping or grading papers or exercising or tutoring a student, all 5 of which are good uses of teacher time, and probably enhance student achievement.

Our belief is that three hours a week of phone calls pay such large dividends in better student effort and behavior, and a better emotional connection for you and your students, that far eclipses the same amount of time spent, say, improving your lesson plans.

6

The Family Speaks No English; Has No Phone; Etc.

We cover this and other logistical issues in Chapter 5. All solvable. One of our charter schools, called Match Community Day, has 84% of families speaking a first language that is not English — moreover, they're spread among 14 different languages. Yet our teachers find ways to communicate with the parents.

7

You're Tired And/Or Hate Phone Calls

It's not that you don't value phone calls in theory. You do. But two things make you want to skip the calls, even if you write it on your to-do list.

First, you are exhausted and passed out on the couch at 7:30 pm. If that's how you feel, consider this. One reason you're tired is simply the raw emotional energy you must spend each day in class putting out fires. If parent phone calls can improve your day-to-day classroom, you'll leave school each day a bit less exhausted.

Second, many of us simply don't like talking on the phone. To our friends. To parents. To spouses or people we date. So of course we don't want to call the parents of our students. Think of this like other things you've had to overcome in order to teach effectively. You probably don't "like" setting clear expectations and holding kids accountable, either, but you've learned to do it because it helps the kids learn. Becoming comfortable with phone calls is the same thing: you just need to resolve yourself to do it as a fundamental building block, just as running sprints is a building block for playing competitive basketball, and practicing scales is a building block for playing music. You have a lot of control over your attitude and mindset here.

8

Weird Faculty Room Vibe

In researching this book, we came across teachers who said some colleagues resented them. "If you call, they'll want me to call, too." Nobody had any good ideas on what to do about this, besides just buckling down and doing what you think is right. And perhaps not plastering advertisements about all the phone calls you've made all over the faculty room walls.

Some teachers will never have heard of this strategy. Others will have tried their version of it and have concluded, "It doesn't work." Our advice: don't be an evangelist (for any particular teaching technique). If a colleague wants to know more, absolutely help — but don't lecture other teachers, nor be intimidated if someone tells you a strategy is a bad idea. Make up your own mind.

9

Fear of Interrupting Family Time

Yes, it's possible you'll interrupt dinner, or bath time, or who knows what. Parents know how to not pick up their phones. They know how to screen calls. Don't worry about this. It's fairly easy to correct. If a parent sounds annoyed or rushed, just ask, "Is there a better time to typically reach you?"

10

Fear of Sounding Inauthentic With Praise

That's legit. It's so much easier to think about the little stuff a student did wrong, or to notice when a student writes a stellar essay or goes way above the call of duty. It feels plain ol' weird to compliment her for doing what you'd expect — paying attention, answering questions, trying hard. You have to make a decision that you believe it is worth pointing this out to a parent. Most phone-calling teachers think of it like this:

A typical parent of a C-average 11-year-old gets pretty much zero positive messaging about their child. I call sometimes to notice the good, even if the good is merely good and not amazing. Noticing "small" good things is part of a larger picture. Doing otherwise is unbalanced, with excessive weight on the bad.

Phone Call Story:
Ray Schleck,
History Teacher

Priscilla was a sharp kid who didn't seem to care what anybody thought of her, therefore everyone kind of ended up liking her. She was kind of a leader in an accidental way.

Teachers at my school didn't call home very much. Our school sent home progress reports every two weeks. So parents were never surprised. If a kid missed homework, an automated call was made by a computer that the student had homework detention. My attitude as a teacher, and that of our school, was that between these two things we do a lot of parent communication.

Priscilla's family also came in for conferences all throughout the year. And they were visibly upset. Part of it was general frustration with Priscilla. They would say things like, "We know she's smart, we don't know why she's not doing her work, we don't know what's going on, we don't know what to do." Typical parent of a rebellious teenager stuff.

But part of it was, "Well this has never happened before. She was fine until now. What is going on in this school that caused these negative changes to happen?" The subtext was: "What are you teachers doing wrong?" They had no trust in us. Some tears. Some accusations. One time the dean had to suggest that Priscilla step out of the meeting.

I just was thinking, 'Why are you, the parent, carrying on in front of your kid? This is a horrible message to be sending...'

In her second year at our school, I was her advisor, and ended up having many phone conversations, usually with Dad. There was a huge uptick in her academic success that seemed to come from the calls. What would we talk about? We usually had about 3 different types of calls:

1 Big assignments coming up made up about 20% of the conversations.

2 A big chunk, maybe 40%, were general mood/behavior updates on Priscilla. Parents reacted well to that, "Okay good to know." Sometimes they would apologize. I would reiterate: "Priscilla's behavior is not a reflection on you guys. Every kid is different, I get it. I know that; you need to know that too. When Priscilla gets in trouble, I know you guys are working really hard at home and that you are doing everything you can on your end. We're all going to keep working on it. Not every day is going to be a good day with Priscilla, that's the deal, I don't blame you guys."

3 The rest were conversations about Priscilla's academic effort. If she wasn't "into" an assignment, she'd openly skip it or put in very little effort. So a lot of the parent conversations were like "Even if Priscilla thinks the assignment is stupid, it's not. Just trust my professional judgment here. The purpose is helping her practice these skills. Beyond that, her refusal to do the work is simply hurting her grade."

Result?

Her second year was a huge improvement. Moreover, her parents didn't complain anymore when they came into school. While I suspect the phone calls were not the only reason — causes are hard to untangle — I'm sure they helped a lot.

THE FOUR TYPES OF PARENT RESPONSES

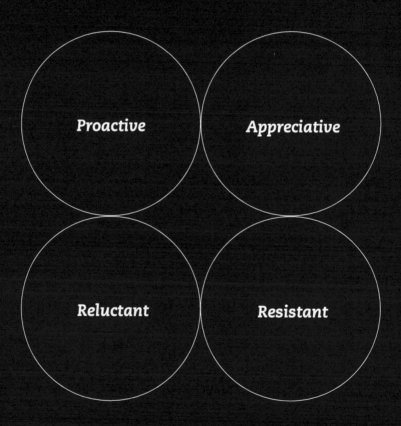

Chapter Three

Skip this chapter if you want. Remember,
Chapter 5 is How To Call. This one deals
with your emotions.

We're not touchy-feely at Match. But this chapter shows our sensitive side. This one deals with your emotions.

Let's get real. Occasionally parents are fun to call. But sometimes — at first, and maybe all year — parents annoy you. Or infuriate you. This will inevitably tempt you to stop communicating with them. In fact, it may also sour you on calling the other parents who you're otherwise fine with.

You may be tempted to label parents as "good" ones and "bad" ones. Don't do that.

You need to communicate well with each parent, without exception.

We want you to enlist all types of parents as partners. Not "faux" partners, where you really treat them like children. Legitimate partners.

Therefore, we've classified parent responses into four types. They just describe how you feel when you talk to a parent. They don't describe the parent.

The same mom may sometimes respond to you in a proactive way, sometimes in a resistant way, and other times in a neutral way. Guess what? You're not the epicenter of her life. Other things are causing her joy and pain.

These categories are oversimplified. We don't want you to think of these as "fixed." These descriptions are not meant to describe any intrinsic parent qualities. You might call them archetypes—each based upon a different type of response a parent might have to a call from their child's school.

Responses can be categorized in one of four ways:

1. Proactive.
2. Appreciative.
3. Reluctant.
4. Resistant.

As you think about these categories, remember to have a "growth mindset," about both yourself, and about a parent. One dad might give Resistant responses for several weeks and then you have a breakthrough, and going forward his responses are Appreciative or even Proactive.

And even without any action by you or other teachers, parent participation may change during the year, or even from one year to the next. People's circumstances change. Jobs — better job, too many jobs, no job. Family — relationships, other kids in the house, sick family members to care for, untreated depression. All of these might affect how a parent responds to a phone call from a schoolteacher.

On the flip side, make sure that you remain "neutral" in how you treat that student in your class. It is tempting to let him get away with more because his Proactive parent is heavily involved in the school. But this is both unfair and damaging to the child. All students should be held to the same high standard, behaviorally and academically.

Response 1 of 4: Proactive

As you talk to some parents, you'll get the sense they often sit with their child at home and help them with homework or studying. If the student is a teenager, the parent might not sit with the kid, but at least ensures something that looks like homework is actually completed. They establish high expectations for their kids: probably rewarding them when met, but willing to punish kids, too (for example, "grounding" a son or daughter who isn't doing assigned essays).

When you call, the Proactive Response is both to do what you hope — show up for conferences, volunteer for field trips, push their kids to try hard — and sometimes even to do more, like ask you for extra material to use with the child at home.

Of course that's gold to the teacher. You'll enjoy a Proactive Response. Your information leads to parent action with the student: sometimes rewards, sometimes punishment, sometimes support.

These parent actions sometimes work and sometimes fail, but at least action is always taken in response to your communication.

As a teacher, when you're fortunate to get Proactive Responses, you sometimes should stretch what you ask for. While a typical teacher phone call focuses on getting their help with the day-to-day objectives of kids completing homework and studying for your class, perhaps you can open the discussion a bit wider towards the kid's overall improvement.

For example, if you are an English teacher and getting Proactive Responses to your phone calls, go ahead and educate these parents about reading levels, choosing books, and encouraging reading, particularly pleasure reading on weekends and during holidays. Imagine if a few specific conversations between a teacher and parent helped a student to develop a one-book-a-month reading habit for the next several years! That's a huge payoff to your student for a few conversations.

If you are a math teacher, you could offer access to different kinds of math drills, puzzles, and games that parents could use with their children.

Science teachers can suggest special weekend or summer enrichment opportunities around the city, at museums and so forth.

If the parent did not herself attend college, you might encourage her to take their kids on college tours. Tours are easy to learn about; you just call up an admissions office. They're free. They're a great way to "manufacture" parent-child dialogue about colleges, and for a parent to communicate that college is important.

Even if the student tells a parent, "I want to go away to college," a visit to a local college can help the student and parent understand different types of colleges. If a student dreams of Georgetown, and you teach in New Orleans or New York, a parent-student visit to Tulane or NYU is still helpful.

2

Response 2 of 4: Appreciative

You call. A parent picks up or phones you back if warranted. You praise a student. The parent passes it along to his son.

If you call with an issue of misbehavior or lack of student effort, an Appreciative response would be to thank you for the information, and that he'd have a word with his kid. That will deter some amount of future misbehavior. However, the urgency of the "shape up" message might not be as high as the Proactive Response we described above.

Again, it's fun to get this response. It's nice to be appreciated.

When you hear appreciation, you should reinforce their support by recognizing the parents' contribution to their student's success. In other words, count them taking your call as legitimate involvement in the student's education. Some parents don't have enough time or "social capital" for kitchen table oversight of studying. When you hear Appreciative responses, don't stop — make communication convenient for these parents by asking them when they want you to call. Make them feel like partners, ask their opinions and ideas for troubleshooting, and listen. Don't overtly or (more likely) subconsciously signal that you are disappointed that they are not being more proactive.

If they seem open it to it, try to move parents who are frequently Appreciative "up" a category to respond more proactively.

How? Gently suggest concrete ways that they can help their kid achieve his dreams.

Sometimes a parent is appreciative but simply lacks specific ideas on how to be more proactive. She may not know how to create a sense of urgency with her daughter, how to push (and examples from other parents may help), how to hold a tearful/angry child accountable, how to get the TV turned off and a book opened, where to go to a museum (and what night is free) and what to do once there, etc. She may not know how to praise her kid, to stop badgering because it comes naturally, to even tell an adolescent "I love you". If that's what is missing — how-to knowledge — you can solve that via conversation.

3

Response 3 of 4: Reluctant

Some parents respond to your calls with reluctance. Here are three ways that non-involvement manifests:

- **Paying lip service.**
- **Trying to get off the phone.**
- **Becoming exasperated with the situation.**

When you hear this, don't get flustered. Many teachers have heard this response early, and then as trust was built, the Reluctance became Appreciation. Sometimes the teacher just misunderstood the parent. Other times, teacher persistence just paid off, and a parent stepped up to the plate. Either way, the obvious message: keep calling, because there's a chance you'll help your student by activating a parent.

Paying Lip Service
Sometimes parents will pay lip service to your requests, and then won't follow through. They will listen to you and tell you what they think you want to hear. But that's it. As a result, their child will continue to struggle with the same issues.

This is a tricky situation. You should not confront parents directly even if they've pledged certain follow-up actions that have not happened. That is absolutely not your place. You're not the teacher of a parent. You're the teacher of a kid.

Instead, continue to call with the intent to keep them informed. Let the parent know when their kid is continuing the concerning behavior, even if you don't believe this information is being used in any productive, direct way.

Sometimes, reluctance just means a parent is unsure about what to do.

Ask: "Is there anything else that we can both do that shows that we mean business? On my end, I have done X... Now I'm going to try Y..."

Ask if they need more information or help on planning out the conversation they'll have with their child. Give suggestions about what you've seen other parents try.

Trying to Get Off the Phone
A parent might respond mono-syllabically, agreeing with you without seeming to hear what you are saying. "Uh-huh. Uh-huh. Yeah. I'll talk to him about it," might be the extent of a phone call.

This is frustrating.

However, you don't know why they want to get off the phone. It may be because they don't like being called, ever. It may be because they are tired and want to relax. It may be because you tend to call when they are trying to put the baby to bed, and he just threw up all over the couch. It may be because you, the teacher, are not particularly helpful and seem judgmental. And frankly, it may be because they don't care enough about their kid's education. But this is rare.

Use light but consistent nudging. As the student continues the (positive or negative) behavior, keep calling the parent. Stay upbeat and positive. Don't show frustration in your tone or word choice. If the issue is a student's negative choices, emphasize your shared concern for the student and his/her education, rather than how much it annoys you when she spills pencil shavings all over your room every day.

Ask questions and give data, such as, "What can we both do to show we mean business? I want to see your child succeed. I know he can. Two weeks ago, he got 100% on three daily quizzes in a row. But his behavior is still very inconsistent. He's had to leave class twice this week. What else can we try?"

Keep calling.

Becoming Exasperated

Some parents, when you call them about a child's misbehavior, may react with complete exasperation. You make a Correction Call, and you hear:
"I know, Mrs. Teacher! Joe does the same thing at home! I've tried everything! He's already on punishment. He can't go out of town to see his grandmother. And no TV. But he's still acting like a crazy person! I just don't know what to do with him anymore!"

This exasperation is understandable. You may feel it, too. Don't give into it. Kids often do change if given the right support. Suggest small steps that both you and the parent can take together.

For example, if a student is backtalking to you when you give him directions, you might say to the frustrated parent: "I had a conversation with Dujuan

about this already. We agreed that if he felt frustrated by a direction I gave him, he would write a note to me and give it to me at the end of class. This way, he can give his point of view without being disruptive. Could you encourage him to keep up with this plan? You could tell him that we both want to see improvement, and that this seems like a fair way for him to improve. Would that be okay?"

If the parent agrees, let her know when you will follow up the call. Continue to follow up with the student and parent until the behavior improves.

If the parent is truly at the end of her rope, she may be disinclined to do any more. "If he wants to get detention every day, that's fine with me," is one thing you might hear from a defeated parent. Again, you should push back against this. Although the parent may be frustrated, she still has a lot of influence over her child. Except in the most extreme circumstances, teenagers do care about what parents do and say. It's not always apparent or obvious to parents, however, that their child really does care (just as it isn't always obvious to teachers).

Start with small goals. In the example above, you might reply,

"Well, I don't think that it would be a very positive experience for him to get detention every day. It might make him give up entirely. I don't think that he really understands the consequences of his impulsive reactions. You have the wisdom and insight that he may not, even if he says he does. Encouragement from you would mean a lot to him deep down, even if he rolls his eyes."

This defeatism about children is more common with parents of high-schoolers. A common refrain:

"It's her life. She doesn't listen to me. She knows the consequences of not doing her work. If she wants to fail, that's her choice."

Again, do not give in. You might say:

"I'm sure that she knows she may fail. But she will still be affected by what you say and do. She's on the brink of making some bad choices, and I DON'T think she totally understands the long-term consequences of failing this class, and I think you can help her with that. I have tried to give her the message about what she needs to do, but I think it would mean a lot coming from you."

Parents need encouragement, just like teachers. You can provide that encouragement.

Make sure to follow up frequently with these parents. When you see improvement in the student, follow up immediately and thank the parent for all their support. This will reinforce whatever they have done and give them more confidence in their parenting and in their child.

Ellie Brown, Social Studies Teacher, describes a parent Reluctantly responding to her phone calls:

"Noah earned detention every day for the first two weeks of school. He was earning small demerits for bad habits such as not meeting directions immediately, not being prepared for class, or getting distracted during instruction. His mother quickly became disinvested in our school's policies and in Noah's teachers who were assigning him the demerits. At this point, she very much fit the description of the exasperated parent. She was punishing Noah at home, had taken away all of his privileges and he was still earning detentions because he wasn't voluntarily misbehaving, it was the product of bad habits."

In this case, the mother first needed to be reassured that

A — Noah was a good kid who was trying as hard as he could and that we recognized that.

B — Our system of holding him to these expectations would ultimately pay off for him in the long run and he would get there in time.

"Finally, I encouraged mom to set small, feasible goals for Noah and to reward him for meeting those goals instead of punishing him for not meeting them."

Most of the phone calls we describe in this book are really short. Quick praise, or quick correction. What follows is unusual: a longer call addressing persistent parent reluctance to engage.

Alison Kelly, English Teacher:

Brenda is a 17-year-old 9th grade student; she's repeating the school year.

"This year she has turned it around, academically at least. Alas, sometimes because she knows the content, she gets bored. Then she starts to be the 'funny one' and has a knack for distracting others."

"I met her mother at the beginning of the school year. It was an IEP meeting to talk about Brenda's recent diagnosis of ADHD. Our introduction was quick and polite. Mom definitely has a lot on her plate. She was also recently laid off from work. Brenda is one of 8 children. It's very understandable that she's less involved with Brenda. She's often exhausted. It's clear she loves her child. But she has very little support."

"My calls are far from perfect, I'll be honest. Her mom wants her to do well. Mom gets very excited when I call to report good grades. She is upset when I give her bad news, but never works with me to form solutions."
"As a result, most of my calls are pretty

short. I do a lot of the talking. I am either so excited with positive news that I ramble, or I am worried that she will get angry about negative news, so I ramble in order to prevent a negative reaction. I'm getting better as I practice."

"Here is a typical call."

Me: Hi Ms. T. It's Ms. Kelly — how are you tonight?

Mrs. T: Good thanks.

Me: I just wanted to give you an update on Brenda's grades and behavior at school this week. I want to start off by saying that she has made a huge improvement this week, and I'm really excited to share it with you! She received 0 demerits this week compared to 10 last week!

Mrs. T: Oh wow!

Me: I know! As a result, all of her grades also went up this week, because she's functioning well in class, taking notes, doing the reading, tackling the problems. It's a positive loop — because she's focused in class, she can do the homework. For example she has had 100% homework completion every day, 92% homework correctness and scored a 103% on her Algebra test — got everything plus the extra credit problems.

Mrs. T: It's about time.

Me: There are only 10 more days left in the semester and I want her to pass all of her classes this semester.

Mrs. T: I would like that too.

Me: Can we come up with a plan to make sure she is getting homework completed every night? What would you suggest we do?

Mrs. T: I would like you to continue to call me to remind her of what she needs to do every night. She forgets.

"Here's what I said at the time: 'Okay.'"

"What would I say now, given my student load?"

Me: It's difficult for me to call you every night. I have many other students. However, I have an idea. I have two students with A averages who always know what is assigned, and they're both friends with your daughter. They're both open to getting calls on their cell phones. In fact I think they like it. What if your first move is to ask Brenda to call them? If you and she don't get what you need, then absolutely call me.

"Would I expect this parent to really follow through? I realize there's a decent chance she will not. Still I feel the call helps. It definitely keeps my relationship with her solid in case things take a turn for the worse with her child's effort and learning, and it has a chance — maybe 50%, maybe 30%, I have no idea — of paying off more directly."

4

Response 4 of 4: Resistant

Some parents will be resistant to you. Sometimes you will hear outright resistance to your communication, particularly if you are the bearer of bad news. They attack the messenger: you, the teacher.

In a call like this, parents will question everything that you do. They will ask about the behavior of other students, rather than focusing on the behavior or academic performance of their child. They may suggest that you are picking on their child. They may make very unflattering suggestions about your motives or values or fairness. You may be called a sexist. A racist. Other –ists.

They may threaten you, either that they'll complain to your principal or even sue you.

(FYI: if this happens, you should inform your principal right away. That way if she or he does get a complaint call from the parent, it won't come out of left field from the principal's point of view).

The hostility sometimes stems from negative interactions with teachers and schools in the past. She is defending her child from what she perceives as an unwelcoming school or an uncaring teacher.

If you anticipate resistance, script out your conversations beforehand, and even practice it out-loud in the mirror or with a friend. That way you sound warm, straightforward, and confident. You're not trying to deceive, but you are trying to avoid subconsciously saying to a parent through tone "I find you to be a really unpleasant person."

Also, the more data you can bring into the conversation, the less suspicious the parent will be that you are "picking on" their child. There's a difference between:

"I had to send out Delia today, she was a handful."

and

"Delia greeted me politely today and she was quite productive in the first 20 minutes of class. She completed all 9 of the assigned problems and got 8 of them right. But then she had a rough 5 minutes. Whoo! She put her head on the desk, snorted when I asked for her focus, muttered some curse words, and slapped her desk loudly with both hands."

Do not take the Resistant Response pushback personally. If you emotionally respond, it will cause you to be defensive. This will make the situation worse.

As The Godfather, Don Corleone, says, "It's not personal, just business." That's what your approach should be. Although — not to contradict ourselves — in Puzo's novel (not the movie), Michael Corleone, the Don's son, has a different view. After he becomes Godfather, Michael says, "It's all personal, every bit of it."

Those mafia dons. Always playing both sides. But Michael C is right, too. A parent who is confronting you will get your pulse racing, and it will mess with your mind a bit. It will sure as heck feel personal! Your job is to keep things even keeled even though you feel under attack.

If parents do respond to you with hostility, stay calm. Ask questions to clarify what they've said. Don't make any judgments (yet) or try to argue. Let them talk as much as they need to. Continue to listen and repeat back in good faith. "I hear you saying X... Is that right?"

Once they acknowledge that you have correctly re-stated their point of view, you can start the conversation over.

First, directly state how much you care about their child and how much you want him or her to succeed. If you can, point to specific things that the student does well. This softens up many parents, because you're signaling that you are not the kind of teacher who simply lumps their child into a category called "Bad Kid."

Next, acknowledge their point of view, i.e., "I can see how it could seem like I'm picking on your son..." Highlight everything they said that you agree with, "You're right, I definitely spent a lot of time by his desk today..."

When you do disagree with them, don't directly challenge their account. Simply describe your own observations. Bring in data. Recite events. Say things like, "Ezra was having a hard time not talking while I was teaching. He turned around three or four times to talk to his friend behind him."

Explain your actions in terms of helping the student, "I found that when I stood near him, he was able to focus better. I wasn't trying to punish him or pick on him. I want all my students to learn as much as possible, and it seemed to help all around when I stood near Ezra."

Sometimes, you may be taken completely off guard with a parent's hostility, and begin to lose your composure. When you feel this: end the conversation, quickly and politely. You want your relationship with the parent to remain professional, and tears or anger will not help.

After letting the parent vent, you can say something like, "You've given me a lot to think about. I will confess I'm taken aback. I'm surprised. I'd like some time to think over what you said. Is there a time tomorrow that we can talk?" This gives you time to decompress.

Note: "I'm surprised" is different from "I'm annoyed as hell because you have GOT to be kidding me. Do you even CARE about your kid?" The latter may flash in your subconscious but you need to keep it there.

If a parent goes so far as to become verbally abusive or threatening, end the call immediately. You interrupt:

"I think this conversation is no longer productive. We can schedule a conversation or meeting for a later time. Thank you, have a good night." Then hang up.

Tell your principal so you can decide next steps.

(Note: This will rarely happen but it's always good to be prepared.)

SIX MOVES THAT WORK

Chapter Four

1   The Praise Call

2   The Correction Call

3   The Check-In Call

4   Text Message To Parent

5   The Summit

6   The Home Visit

There's never enough time. So, following are four quick moves you can execute to build relationships. (Plus a couple that take longer.)

1

The Praise Call

In a Praise Call, a teacher describes in some detail a positive choice made or a goal met by the student.

Praise Calls are useful to use with all categories of parents and students, but particularly valuable with kids like Troubled Tom and Driving Me Crazy. The parents of these kids are used to negative calls from school. They may be resigned to perceiving their child as a "bad kid."

The Praise Call here allows you to break the basic negative cycle. If a struggling kid has a good day, nothing is more likely to help him have a second good day than a phone call to try to "lock in" the good behavior. You're narrating the positive.

Of course parents of your well-behaved students, whether their academic level is strong or weak, are often overlooked. They probably rarely get much direct teacher contact. It is vital that you take time to recognize these students, too, to reinforce their positive choices. Not only do they deserve that recognition (every kid does), but if you do, they'll try even harder in your class and possibly enlist some other kids to follow suit.

Notes on Praise

Three guidelines: Any praise you give should be specific, child-centered, and effort-driven.

Praise Must Be Specific
Instead of saying, "Joe put a lot of effort into studying this week," you want to give lots of details about what happened. Here's what you might say instead:

"Joe put a lot of effort into studying this week. He had his homework done every day. He came in after school twice to get help with his math homework. He stayed for 45 minutes each time and worked really hard to understand everything, not just get the answers. As a result of all his hard work and good thinking, he got an A on his Friday quiz!"

By giving details, you are showing that you really pay attention when the student does something well. You're making the praise more authentic. And you also give the student or parent more time to enjoy hearing about his good work.

Fake praise is easily detected. Call it the way you see it. Certainly with some kids you will need to reflect a little to find things that merit authentic praise, but you should never manufacture false praise — it's counterproductive.

Praise Should be Child-Centered, not Teacher-Centered
This means reduce your own judgment from the statement of praise. Instead of saying, "He got 100% on his test!

I'm so proud of him!," you should say, "He got 100% on his test! He should be so proud of himself! I believe his choice to stay for the Thursday after-school review session paid off."

It's a small thing, but it matters.

"I'm so proud of you" can send the message that the student's self-image should depend on others' judgment of him or her. "Be proud of yourself," on the other hand, sends the message that the student's judgment of himself is more important.

Praise Effort and Choices
Kids gravitate to "fixed" views of intelligence. Kid A is smart. Kid B is dumb. Children internalize this, about themselves.

As a teacher, you need to help kids (and their parents) internalize the notion that academic success often comes from effort and decision-making than simply from aptitude. You do that by being (unusually) explicit in what you call to praise, directly linking actions (which a kid does control) to outcomes.

This helps students develop independent judgment about their own actions, which they can rely on even when the teacher or parent is not around.

Example Of A Praise Call

A

Greet

B

Time Check

C

State Reason for Call

D

Decide Next Steps

E

Goodbye

Ms. Harper: Hello?

You: Hi, Ms. Harper. It's Ms. Longfellow, Jacob's English teacher.

Ms. Harper: Oh, yes, hello.

You: Great to hear your voice, I just need two minutes of your time. Is this a good time, or would you like me to call back late

Ms. Harper: Oh no, this is fine.

You: I called to tell you about a great thing Jacob did today. Jacob was really focused in class today. Every time I looked over, he was following directions or tracking the other kids. The first time was when I asked everyone to get out their books — he was the first one ready! When another student answered a question, he quickly swiveled in his chair to listen to what the other kids ha to say. As a result, he was consistently read to work, he participated a lot, and he was able to do his classwork without any help. His behavior showed a lot of determination

Ms. Harper: Well, that's wonderful. I'm so glad to hear it.

You: Yes, me too. Would you pass on the compliment to him? I want him to know exactly what he was doing well so he can keep doing it! And I want him to know that we notice when he's doing well.

Ms. Harper: I certainly will pass it on. Thank you.

You: I'll speak with you soon.

Ms. Harper. Take care.

Ms. Harper: You too. Bye now.

2

The Correction Call

In the Correction Call, you describe something that the student needs to improve. Then, you help the student and parent envision what improvement would specifically look like, and what steps can be taken immediately to begin this process.

You want to always frame these conversations around the fact that you care about this individual student and want to see him or her succeed. The point is to communicate that you care, and that the conversation you are having is not about punishment, but about problem-solving for the good of everyone.

Example Of A Correction Call

Correction Calls follow the same 5-part format as Praise Calls:

A Greeting

You: Hi, Ms. Cook, it's Mr. Awesome, Nash's math teacher.

Ms. Cook: Hello.

You: How are you doing?

Ms. Cook: I'm well, and yourself?

You: Doing just fine, thank you.

B Time Check

You: I need 5 minutes of your time to talk about Nash. Is this a good time for you?

Ms. Cook: Yes, it's fine.

C State Reason For Call

You: I'm calling because I'm concerned about Nash. He is missing a lot of what I'm teaching because he's talking to neighbors. Today I made a point to take some notes on the situation. I counted three different times when he was talking to his neighbor while I was teaching. I tried some different strategies. I reminded the whole class. I redirected him specifically with a tap on the shoulder. And after those things, I give him demerits when he does this — in fact I've given him five total in the last two days. But it doesn't seem to make a difference.

This behavior is hurting him because he's not hearing parts of the lesson, and I can see that reflected on his homework — his homework accuracy has been lower. He's also preventing his classmates around him from hearing all of the lesson.

D Discuss And Decide Next Steps

You: Is there anything that you know of that is going on with Nash that might make him especially distracted in class?

Ms. Cook: No, no, everything is fine. He's just social. Always has been.

You: Ok well what I'm looking for is for Nash to focus on what I'm saying during the lesson and be silent unless it's a time to talk within the lesson. I need your help to make that happen. Do you think you could speak to him about this issue?

Ms. Cook: Of course I will! He shouldn't be talking over you like that. He knows better.

You: I want him to know that this is an issue that can hurt him as well as other students. Could you mention that to him as well?

Ms. Cook: Yes. He needs to get his grades up. And those other kids around him don't need to be distracted either.

You: Ok. I will call you tomorrow to let you know how he does. (If things were better tomorrow, you'd call with a Praise Call).

Ms. Cook: I would appreciate that.

E Goodbye

You: Ok, great. Thank you Ms. Cook.

Ms. Cook: Thank you. Goodbye now.

3

The Check-In Call

Check-in Calls are a time for you to see how a **student** is doing with his or her classwork or homework. It's an academic check-in, rather than praise or correction. Typically you'd speak with the **student** before the parent, if possible.

A Greeting

Maria: Hello?

You: Hi Maria, this is Ms. Pebo. How are you?

Maria: I'm fine.

B Time Check

You: Good. Listen, I probably need 10 minutes of your time. Is now good?

Maria: Yeah, that's fine.

C State Purpose Of Call

You: Okay. Listen, I'm calling to check o how you're doing with your homework today. It seemed like you struggled wit the classwork today, and you got a few questions wrong on the Ticket to Leave Do you find this stuff kind of difficult?

Maria: Yeah, I didn't really get it.

You: That's ok, it happens. Have you done your English homework yet?

Maria: No, not yet.

You: Let's take a look at it together.

Maria: Ok, hold on let me get it out... uh...(30 second of shuffling noises) Ok here it is.

You: Why don't you start by reading the directions.

Maria: "Read the newspaper article. Then answer the 5 questions which follow. Make sure you go back to the passage and underline the evidence you used to answer each question."

D Discuss and Decide Next Steps

You: Right, exactly. So what I want you to do is read to yourself right now. I'm going to write an email while you're doing that. I figure it'll take you a few minutes.

Maria: Ok. [She reads for 5 minutes.] I'm done.

You: Tell me about what you read.

Maria: Well it's this passage about where popcorn came from, that the Native Americans used to eat it.

You: Good. Now let's go on to question #1. Read it to me.

Maria: One. Some Native Americans used to eat popcorn for breakfast. What did they eat it with? Oh here it is: "Some Native Americans used to put their popcorn in milk and eat it for breakfast."

You: Great! What should you do now?

Maria: Answer the question.

You: Not yet. Before you answer, what should you do in the passage?

Maria: Oh, underline the evidence.

You: That's right. What could you do to help yourself remember?

Maria: Maybe I could write myself a note on the side of the page.

You: Great idea! Ok, did you underline it?

Maria: Yeah. Now I'm going to answer the question.

You: Good. So what are you going to remember to do on the rest of the questions?

Maria: Underline the evidence in the passage.

You: Great job Maria. Keep it up. I really appreciate you working on this tonight. Taking just a little bit of extra time to learn will help you a lot. I'll probably ask you about underlining evidence in class tomorrow, so be ready, ok?

Maria: Ok.

E Connect With Mom

You: Is your Mom there?

Weird noises that typically happen when phone gets handed off.

Mom: Huh?

You: It's Ms. Pebo, Maria's teacher.

Mom: Hi.

You: I just wanted to let you know I had a good conversation with Maria, and she said she'll spend the next half hour or so working on homework for my class. She has to read a few articles and answer questions.

Mom: Got it.

You: Thanks for all your support.

Mom: Bye.

4

Text Message To Parent

This only works with parents with whom you have rapport. There are two versions.

Praise Text: "Justin did nice work on his quiz. 95! *Mr. Goldstein"

Reminder Text: "Rose has a big chemistry test this Friday. 45 minutes studying/night would help. *Mr. Goldstein."

Don't use texts for concerns — call instead.

5

The Summit

The Summit is an emergency, in-person meeting with parent and student both present. It is scheduled after you have tried all different kinds of interventions with a student and parent, but nothing seems to be working. Often it lasts from 30 minutes to an hour (or more).

The Summit is a chance for the teacher, the parent, student, possibly a colleague, and hopefully the principal to sit down all together and create a plan for how to help the student.

You can use phone calls to build rapport, phone calls to schedule a summit, and phone calls after a summit to reinforce what was said. But you can't really easily have a phone Summit.

Ellie Brown, a teacher, describes the interplay between in-person and phone calls:

> *I've had some success with the in-person meeting, which then sets the table for future phone conversations. Skyla's mom deeply distrusted all of the 5th grade teachers. We called a meeting with mom, Skyla, and all of her teachers. When mom could see how we interacted with Skyla, hear everyone's perspective, and see how well we knew her daughter, her opinion of us completely shifted. She began to trust our motivations and Skyla shifted from a C student who*

earned detention three times a week to a B+ student who only occasionally earned detention. Sometimes even the phone calls can lose that personal touch, and when that happens, an in-person meeting can restart the relationship.

If parents won't come into school, offer to do a home visit. In-person communication allows you to observe the parent and student's body language and interactions. You get a better sense of what their relationship is like, which can give you insight into the child. However, your body language and your relationship to the child are also being observed. Make sure that you are dressed professionally for this meeting, and appear confident, prepared, and caring. Make eye contact with parents and students when you're talking. Be warm but unapologetic about your high expectations for the child. This may be the first time parents are meeting you, and it's an important impression to make.

Let your principal know about the meeting. If she's "good," ask her to be there. The presence of the principal is typically quite helpful: it allows you to listen better, not feeling like you have to always be the one with the next thing to say.

You can also invite another teacher to the meeting if they are having similar problems with the student. Be careful, however, not to have too many people. Some parents may feel intimidated or defensive when they are confronted with four or five people all talking about the negative choices their child is making. You want them to feel like your partner, not your enemy.

The meeting needs to be serious, formal, and urgent. Before the meeting, create an objective and an agenda for the meeting. Be sure to put a place on the agenda for parent and student input.

Follow the steps below.

Step One.

Call parents and set up the meeting. Make sure you tell them the objective of the meeting, and what it is about. Make sure to emphasize that it is a problem-solving conference, to put them at ease that you will not be attacking their parenting or their child. Also be sure to mention which other teachers or administrators may be attending.

Step Two.

When parents first arrive, genuinely thank them for taking their time to come in. This is most likely a stressful experience for them, since their child is not doing what he/she is supposed to do. Being gracious and welcoming will help put them at ease that you are not going to be attacking their parenting or their child.

Once everyone is assembled, you should sit down together in a quiet room. Hand out sheets with aims/agendas to everyone present.

Step Three.

Start the conversation by highlighting something positive about the student. This will let the parents, and student, know you care about him and recognize his potential.

Step Four.

Then, either describe the problematic situation or ask the student to describe it. Use your judgment as to whether the student would be honest and receptive in such a role. If not, you should describe the situation yourself. Identify the negative consequences that result from the student's behavior.

Bring as much data to the conversation as possible. Examples of behavior data might be: demerit logs, weekly progress reports, class notes, your phone log, number of detentions, or any other "numbers" you have. Data is helpful because it is a neutral source. If parents are at all wary about the quality of your judgment and fairness, you can back yourself up with the data.

Step Five.

Solicit information from the student and parents.

You can ask questions such as:
- Has this been a problem for the child before?
- If so, what was done about it?
- Was it effective?
- Does the child have this problem at home?
- Who was the child's best teacher?
- What did he/she do for the student that was effective?
- What do you do at home that helps the child work through difficulties?

Step Six.

Brainstorm goals for the student. Choose one. Then brainstorm strategies that the student, parents, and teacher can use to help the student reach the goal. Write it all up. Review it and make sure everyone agrees to what was decided. Have the student and parent sign the document, and then sign it yourself.

Next Steps.

After this meeting, send your department chair, dean, or principal an email detailing the progression of the student's issue, the documentation you have written up, and the possibility of administrative intervention.

If the student begins improving AT ALL, send praise to her and her parents right away. Make a big deal out of it. If the student begins to slip, use a quick correction call to remind her of the goal and the strategies to use, and let her parents know right away. Continue to monitor the student's behavior.

If the student reaches the established goal, make a BIG deal of it. Changing one's behavior significantly is very difficult, and succeeding in doing so is impressive! Make sure the student and her parents know this!

If the student still does not reach the goal, it is time for more drastic measures. Talk to your principal first, as your school may have a policy for a situation like this. The principal's suggestions may include having a parent sit with the child in class for a day to observe the problem in action or conducting a home visit.

6

The Home Visit

Home Visits are reserved for those students who continue to struggle and struggle, despite tight parent-teacher communication and a Summit meeting.

The Home Visit is a collaboration between a teacher and parent to emphasize the seriousness of the student's difficulties in school.

While Home Visits sound daunting, they often turn out to be very powerful and informative. If done right, they can cement your relationship with the student and parent forever. Very few students have ever had a teacher come to their houses. The power of seeing you, sitting in their house, with their parents, can have quite an effect. It sends several messages:

1 I'm not going to give up on you—I will do whatever it takes for you to succeed.

2 What we are doing is important enough that I am taking the time to come to your house.

3 Your parents and teachers work together, as one, to make sure you get a good education and great opportunities in life.

All these messages combined are quite potent.

To set up a Home Visit, first call the student's parents. Give data to explain how the student is still struggling with his/her behavior, despite the agreement outlined in the Summit.

Explain that you think a good next step might be another meeting, this time in the home. Lay out your reason—that Home Visits send 3 powerful messages to children. Make this point quickly. You don't want parents thinking you are coming to check up on them. Emphasize that you are willing to schedule around their free time, and inform them that another teacher will come with you.

When you go on the Home Visit, you should have another teacher or staff member with you. This is not just to put you more at ease, it is also to shield you from any possible kind of accusation that might be leveled against you (though this type of thing only happens very rarely, it's better safe than sorry), and for personal safety.

While you may be nervous, after the first Home Visit, you may actually look forward to doing them. Many teachers describe breakthroughs, where they eat with the family, meet Grandma and Uncle Moe, and suddenly the relationship with the student blossoms.

ESTABLISHING A PHONE CALL ROUTINE

(and Other Logistics)

M	T
W	Th
F	Sa
Su	

Chapter Five

Now's the part where you have a
choice to make. What's your routine?

August and September Phone Calls

There is a big advantage to "front-loaded" introductory phone calls in August (if you can get your student roster) or the first two weeks of September. These are 5-minute calls.

You're hitting the main themes:

My name is X. I care about your kid. I'm going to push your kid, I think she can do it. You should call or visit anytime. I will check in with you by phone a few times during the year. Any questions. Again, my name is X. Thank you.

The advantage? You get to make a positive call before any need for correction calls can even arise. You "win" the race. No parent likes his first teacher call to be from someone who is criticizing his son or daughter. Avoid that with an intro call.

Choosing a Routine During The Year: High Dose, Medium Dose, Or Low Dose?

Compare phone calls to exercise and other routines. Studies show that a daily routine for just about anything has a certain power, because it takes away the discomfort of pondering, each day, whether you'll do X or skip X. You just do it.

Ad hoc never works. Trust us. If you don't lock in a *routine*, you're not going to be making proactive praise calls. Then you'll find when you want

to call to enlist a parent's help, you have no relationship capital. The parent won't know who the heck you are, and she's more likely to resist you.

Considering Various Routines

There are two things in play here. How many kids you teach. How much time you want to invest.

If you're an elementary school teacher you probably "only" have 20 to 40 kids total. If you're a middle or high school teacher, though, you probably have 60 to 180 total students. Let's examine the three plans — high, medium, and low phone call dosage.

A High Dose Phone Call Routine

Front-loaded introductory calls in August (if you can get your student roster) or the first two weeks of September. 180 * 5 minutes. That's 15 hours, or one hour a night for two straight weeks.

You're hitting the main themes:

My name is X. I care about your kid. I'm going to push your kid, I think she can do it. You should call or visit anytime. I will check in with you by phone a few times during the year. Any questions. Again, my name is X. Thank you.

This is a September "race". You want to have a positive call before any need for correction calls can even arise. Then you settle into your routine for the rest of the year.

Typically this routine makes phone calls happen a little bit every night.

6 Praise Calls Per Night, Sunday to Thursday (30 minutes total)

That comes to 30 calls a week. If you stick to this plan with 180 kids, a parent will hear from you every 6 weeks, or about 3 times a school year. If you are an elementary school teacher with 30 students, it means you can reach every parent EVERY week, which is amazing.

We suggest skipping Friday calls for two reasons. First, the payoff is lower, since kids won't be in class the next day. Second, you should be having a margarita.

In this plan, you also make one Correction Call Per Night, Sunday to Thursday.

Some teachers make extra correction and praise calls on Sunday, because of the nature of a "clean slate" for a new week, and the desire to set kids up for success.

7 phone calls a night * 5 minutes = 35 minutes each Mon, Tue, Wed, Thursday = 140 minutes/week.

10 calls on Sunday * 5 minutes = 50 minutes/week.

"Buffer Zone" time just for returning calls, updating numbers, longer than expected chats = 50 minutes/week
High Dose Total = 240 minutes per week, or 4 hours per week.
What's the Payoff?

What if these 4 hours per week make a 20% improvement to your happiness and success during the 25 hours per week you're teaching the kids? That seems like a fairly large payoff.

B Medium Dose Phone Call Routine

Here your routine is just 30 minutes per night, Sunday to Thursday. It may be while you're driving home (be careful). That's enough time for 3 or 4 Praise Calls, and one Correction call.

C Low Dose Phone Call Routine

Some teachers like to bang it all out in one 90-minute Sunday session. If possible, combine this with a long walk around the neighborhood. It'll keep you relaxed. You can pepper in 15 to 20 rapid-fire praise calls in 60 minutes. Grab a friend and "compete." Leave the final 30 minutes to make Correction Calls or any that need more time to listen.

Other Logistics

1 Where To Call From

Some teachers do this heading home in their car or on the bus. Hard to take notes.

Some go for a walk (we encourage this).

Some sit at a desk or on the couch; this is easiest if you're going to take notes on the calls, or refer to notes.

2 Parents Who Do Not Speak English

Parents who do not speak English, of course, can be in any of these 4 categories. Generally, you will find that you can communicate reasonably well with them simply by using 3-way calling on your cell phone.

The translator? Four choices:

1. A middle or high school student often does the translating for his parent. While you may wonder if the translation is being done accurately, kids are usually pretty good about this — even the "Correction Calls!"

2. Another option is a family member (cousin, older sibling) who is fluent. You get his/her cell number early in the year and establish whether they're willing to translate calls all year.

3. A third option is a volunteer that you befriend who likes to talk on the phone. Your sister's Brazilian nanny; your buddy's colleague at the consulting company; your sorority sister who is still in college — all of these folks may be volunteers in waiting.

4. Another option is bilingual parent in your school who wants to make a time commitment. If you happen to teach in a school where many parents speak the same language (Spanish, Portuguese, Cape Verdean Creole, etc), you can sometimes arrange for a big Sunday phone call session as a routine, and then take the translator to brunch as a thank you.

You can also buy an excellent interpreter for 3-way calls. The price of these services is falling rapidly, and some schools are willing to pay. These services are changing so fast, it's probably best to just Google "interpreter services" so you have up to date information.

Putting It All Together
David Collier

My routine is I make phone calls 3 nights per week. Monday, Thursday and Sunday evening. I make anywhere between 12–20 calls per night. Add it up, I hit about 40–50 kids per week.

I had started on a nightly schedule. Then I realized Tuesday and Wednesday don't work for me, as I'm late at school doing planning. My guess is most teachers will need to tinker with their phone call routine, wherever they start. So the best advice is just pick something, try it, jump in.

Usually the high priority calls that I try to knock out first are calls of students who had difficulty in class. And for these, after I chat with a parent, I'll ask to speak to the kid, even for 30 seconds.

I have a schedule of 14 kids that I have to call on Monday, Thursday and Sunday nights. I systematically call these kids so I make sure to keep in touch with everyone. Then I keep 4 or 5 spots open for kids I want to check in on because of what just happened that day. So that means I get to my entire roster of 90 kids once every two weeks.

I'll have two great weeks where I hit everyone, and one week where I slack off a bit. I notice the difference and try to get back on the wagon. A few calls I get done during my drive home. Others I make at home. Usually do it in front of the TV on mute, a football game if I can find one. Sometimes I go into my room if a roommate is downstairs. Our school gives us a cell, and so I use that phone and have all the numbers programmed into the phone, so dialing is easy.

Usually I can knock out 12–14 calls in one hour, so 5 minutes per call. Usually I don't have notes. I'll pull up a couple of their exit ticket grades on my computer, or I'll think back to how they did in class that day, and mention any general trends I've noticed. I try to take 10–15 seconds before I dial to think of a couple of behaviors I saw in class, and their exit ticket grades. After the call, I jot notes. Our school has an online system where we log the information.

Chapter Six

The other 20 things you were wondering
about parent phone calls.

1

What if a parent doesn't call me back?

Don't take it personally.

Try calling at different times during the day. Parents may have an unusual work schedule and you may be able to reach them at a different time.

Leave clear, polite, brief messages. In the voice message, state that you would like the parent to call you back as soon as possible so you can work together to help the student. Sounding angry, frustrated, or annoyed will not help in your effort to contact them. Make sure to leave your number and several different times they can easily reach you. Give them at least two full days to respond to your voicemail before you try again, unless the matter is urgent.

Make sure you have the right number. Ask other teachers if they have alternate numbers. Ask the student for the number.

Send a note home with the student. Set it up so the student's lunch/recess/free time depends on her returning the note with a signature from the parent, so you know it was delivered.

Find out if the parent drops off the student. If so, you can try to meet them outside to talk.

Ask for help. If you believe that a parent is deliberately not calling you back, ask the other teachers if they have a good relationship with the parent. They may be able to help you figure out what is going on. Finally, ask your principal for help contacting the parent.

2

What if a parent asks for parenting advice?

Parents who are frustrated or "at the end of their rope" with their child's behavior may ask you, "What do you think I should do?" In this situation, you want to be cautious, as you do not want to be responsible for the results. If you're not a parent, you might say:

"You're asking me for advice on how to parent, and I'm not a parent myself. I know this is a common problem for kids, so you may want to ask kids of parents his age what they do."

"Well, I'm not a parent, so I'm not sure. But I have seen some parents do [insert strategy]. Other parents have tried [insert strategy]."

If you are a parent, you should be conservative about what you share. You might agree that parenting is extraordinarily challenging. Your status as a parent grants you a certain privilege to convey empathy. But don't share too many details of your personal situation—every child is different and you need to ensure the focus of the conversation remains your student.

3

Why are you so specific in shooting for calls that are 2 to 5 minutes?

We sort of made that number up, but it seems reasonable. Ten minutes seemed too long — you simply won't have that much to say most of the time. Thirty seconds seemed too short and tends to feel abrupt. So we picked some numbers in the middle. Keep in mind it's going to average out to 2–5 minutes per call, so you'll have some 30 second and some 10 minute calls in there too. Our larger point is you can accomplish a lot with several short "touches" rather than thinking of phone calls as complex, long conversations.

4

What if a parent is unloading problems on me and I can't get a word in?

This is a tough one. Sometimes, a parent needs to unload something, and will really appreciate being listened to respectfully. At other times, it may not be helpful for either of you to go on and on about something negative.

Use your judgment.
You could gently cut into the parent's rant and say, "That sounds really hard," and then try to shift the conversation toward a more productive topic. Or you could wait until the end of the rant and say the same thing.

You'll just have to use your judgment. Be compassionate.

5

What if I'm getting really frustrated with children and feel the parents are at fault?

Sometimes, when parents aren't cooperating as much as you'd like, and their children are frustrating you, it is tempting to bash parents and blame them for the issues in the class. Don't.

If you just need to let off a little steam, talk to a friend or colleague.

Even there, however, don't let yourself blame parents for difficult things happening in your classroom. It is self-defeating.

6

What if the parent starts literally yelling at their kid while I'm on the phone?

Parents yell at students in front of other people because A) they feel embarrassed that someone is calling their child out for his behavior, B) they are frustrated at their child, C) they want to show that the problem does not stem from leniency in the home, and/or d) they're not sure what else to do at that particular moment to express their disapproval.

To assist the parents in undoing this cycle, you can do two things: A) come up with an improvement plan before you make the phone call, and B) start out the phone call by acknowledging what the student is doing well and attributing it in part to parental influence. Sometimes you're stretching to find what he's doing well, but it's okay.

Before the call, ask yourself, "How can this child improve in the area I'm calling about? What is it that I want the parent to do to help the child improve? What is my role in helping the child improve?"

When you first reach the parent, say something like, "I'd like to talk with you for five minutes about _____. Is this a good time? Okay, great. I'd like to just talk over the situation with you first, and then we can bring in _____ to talk. Is that okay? Great."

First, you acknowledge things that the child (and, therefore, the parent) is doing well. "First of all, I wanted to let you know Carlos has been a really active participant in class the last two weeks. He is obviously an enthusiastic math student. Has he always been so full of zest?" Something like this will make the parent feel less defensive and frustrated when you get to the negative part.

Next, to introduce the correction conversation, you might say, "Carlos has been struggling in class lately with _____. Today, for example, he _____. I have some thoughts for what you and I can do, and what he can do, to help him improve in this area. I'd like to run these by you and get your input before we talk to Carlos about it."

At this point, you have signaled several times to the parent that you do not wish for the student to be brought in and scolded at that point. If the parent still wants to yell at his or her child, there's not a whole lot you can do, except to say, "Actually, Ms. _____, I was hoping that you and I could talk about Carlos first. I think that would be much more productive at this point."

7

What if a parent is punishing their kid really severely for really minor behavioral infractions?

The issue here is usually that you, as a teacher, believe a certain parent is calibrating consequences to actions in an inappropriately harsh way. That is, some parents take drastic steps when a child receives even one demerit. The child is terrified of getting a low level behavioral consequence, like a 'demerit' or even a 'warning.

We've seen two versions of this. Sometimes the parent is just way too heavy on consequences. If that's your conclusion, then your correction phone calls may be counterproductive, and stick with praise calls.

Other times this kind of situation occurs with a parent who is new to the idea of giving small consequences for small misbehaviors. Emphasize that the purpose of these consequences is to help students change and improve their behavior. Explain that one demerit does not trigger a consequence at school and that therefore it should probably not trigger one at home.

Instead, come up with a goal for the student's behavior at school with the parent. This will depend on the student's starting point for behavior. The parent can then decide the consequences for not meeting the goal and the rewards (if any) for meeting it.

Re-calibrating the parent's discipline system to the school's will help the student to accept the school's system without fear of parental punishment.

As for the specific consequences the parent gives, that is up to his discretion, including spanking for younger kids. Unless there appears to be abuse going on in the home, or indiscriminate physical punishment, it is a parent's right to physically discipline his child. You just want to make sure that what the parent is doing at home supports, rather than undermines, the discipline system at school, which hopefully tilts heavily towards noticing the positive.

8

How do you distinguish between "lip service" and "responsive" parents?

The only difference between these two categories of parents is in whether or not they follow through with what they say they'll do.

Usually, you'll be able to tell which of your kids have lip service parents and which have reactive-but-supportive parents, because the latter students will usually change their behavior to some degree after you call, whereas the former students will not be affected by your phone call.

Parents who pay lip service but don't act according to your call may have a variety of different reasons for not acting. They may not be home very much when their child is home, so they don't get the opportunity for extended check-ins. They may have other, more serious issues going on in their lives, such as a sick parent. Or they might feel that they have limited influence over their child, and they use it only for the "big fish," such as keeping them from hanging out with the wrong kids. Therefore, be patient with lip service parents, and continue calling them and brainstorming different ways you can collaborate to help the student.

9

What if a parent doesn't think his child has behavior problems and blames you for problems in class?

This means the parent is giving a resistant response, as we describe in Chapter 3. As with other resistant parents, use data to bolster your argument, make sure other teachers are calling with the same issues (if they are happening in other classes), and call to praise as well as correct.

For example, if you tell the parent, "Daphne got into arguments with three different students today. The other three students did not get into arguments with any other students," then it's going to be difficult for the parent to blame you or the other students for this one, though he or she might try. Continue relationship-building with the parent and student. Eventually you will see some success.

10

What if a parent complains about other teachers to me?

The best thing to do in this situation is to avoid getting directly involved in the relationships between the other teachers and the parent. Don't try to defend the teacher against what the parent is saying. At the same time, don't agree with the parent.

If the other teacher is someone that is open to parent communication, you can connect them. While still on the phone with the parent, you can say, "I know that _____ really cares about your daughter's success. I think that if you let her know that you feel this way, she would want to work with you to fix the situation. I'll let her know that she should call you."

At this point, they may continue to complain about the teacher, or tell you that talking to her won't help. Listen quietly without agreeing. When she finishes, continue with the same message, "Again, I know _____ would want to work this out with you personally."

If you teach in a school with some colleagues that you believe are not going to try to communicate with an unhappy parent, you're in a little bit of a bind. It's probably not productive to engage too much. "I really can't speak for Mr. X, I hope you understand."

After the conversation, go directly to the teacher or teachers involved, and the principal, and tell them what the parent told you. Don't be overdramatic. Simply pass along that XYZ parent is frustrated, that you explained you know Ms. Other Teacher(s) cares, and ask if they phone can phone the parent that night.

11

What if a parent doesn't speak English?

See chapter five.

12

What do I say to parents if I've tried "everything" with a difficult kid and it's just not working?

Yes, some students are really challenging. Sometimes, though, what they don't need is a new strategy. Sometimes they just need the same strategy applied consistently for a prolonged period of time.

So start out with one simple plan (i.e. reminders in class, track demerits daily and call home each night to report, congratulate every time he has a good class or day) and then stick to it for at least two weeks. Call the parent during the two weeks to reaffirm both of your commitment to the plan, even if the student is still struggling. If you see any improvement by the end of the two weeks, continue with the plan. Some kids just take awhile to change.

13

What do you tell the parent when you see a student putting in tons of effort and still failing?

The student in this case probably has a severe skill deficiency. The parent needs to know this ASAP.

Talk to your principal and the other teachers in your grade. Consider having the parent in for a Summit.

If you decide to go with a meeting, have materials ready beforehand. Give the parent evidence as to how severe the child's skill deficiency is. Lay out a plan of action for the student (tutoring, calling teachers at night, attending extra help sessions, studying a lot for tests). If the skill deficiency is so severe that the student is likely to fail the grade, let the parent know now, and consider a special education referral.

14

How do you overcome an inclination to be apologetic in conversations with parents?

Teachers feel apologetic when they perceive a call home to parents as an attempt to punish the child or exact retribution for bad behavior. It feels to you like you're lumping pressure and stress onto the parent, so you feel bad. In order to feel better about corrective phone calls, you need to re-frame how you think about them. They are not about the past. They are not about punishment or about making the parent stressed or getting back at the student.

You make phone calls because you care about the student and you want to help him or her improve.

If you have a reason to call, the student is not making good choices for herself and needs to change course. The best people to help her with that are her parents and you. Working together, you can be an even greater force to help her change and be successful.

When you look at phone calls in this light, you shouldn't feel the need to apologize, and you won't be condescending because you're asking the parents to partner with you to help their children.

15

Is email a proper substitute for phone calls if the parent prefers it?

If the parent asks to be contacted that way, you can definitely use it. However, it's not a pure substitute, as it makes the back and forth of verbal conversation harder to achieve.

16

Should I ask about how the parent is doing at the beginning of a phone call?

You can if you'd like. Some parents appreciate the courtesy; others just want you to get to the point; a few "over-answer" that question and ramble on. You'll quickly be able to tell which is which.

17

What if a parent feels like the home visit is to check in on them? Won't they be defensive?

Not if you set up the home visit with the parent well beforehand. You have to frame it as a strategy to benefit the student. Explain to the parents that kids can be powerfully affected by the power of seeing you sitting in their house with their parents. It tells the student that:

A   I'm not going to give up on you—I will do whatever it takes for you to succeed.

B   What we are doing is important enough that I am taking the time to come to your house.

C   Your parents and teachers work together, as one, to make sure you get a good education and great opportunities in life.

If you frame the home visit as a way to reach the child, parents are unlikely to object.

18

Are home visits possible for all categories of parents?

In our experience, parents even of high school seniors have felt positive about home visits. It's much more convenient for them than having to come to the school.

19

How do you effectively utilize the other person you bring along on a home visit?

The other person should be a teacher or school official who interacts with the student. You can lead the discussion, and this other person can provide additional comments and insight. Sometimes they will just be there to provide support and make you feel more comfortable.

20

What if on the phone call, or what I overhear makes me fear abuse by a parent or relative, or some other serious issue?

You treat it like any other information that makes you fear abusive parent behavior. That is, bring your concerns to your principal immediately. When you do, try to separate your judgment from the facts. "Mrs. K has made several remarks that made me feel uneasy. For example, she said X."

In most states, there are rules for principals that trigger automatic reporting to state agencies; moreover, good principals will bring a wealth of experience and concern to each such case. Each state has different rules about what to do.

Here in Massachusetts, the general idea is that "suspected abuse" must be reported to the Department of Children and Families. However, there's a lot of nuance for the principal in deciding how best to ascertain if something meets the criteria of "suspected abuse." The important thing is that you give your principal all the relevant facts of the situation (less your judgments, more what you've directly observed or been told).

ACKNOWLEDGMENTS

This book was a group effort.

First, thank you to every teacher and tutor from Match Charter School over the years. You do the real work.

Second, the notion of calling parents was not invented by us. That would be ridiculous. Tens of thousands of teachers have invented many ways to communicate with parents. All we're doing is trying to write it down, so that if you want to do it, you understand how, when, and why.

Third, the good folks at Match Teacher Residency and the Charles Sposato Graduate School of Education all contributed to this book. Randall Lahann, Erica Winston, Laura Mahajan, Laura Hankin, Scott McCue, Orin Gutlerner, Veronica Gentile, Ross Trudeau, Colin Bottles, Kenny Wang, Kat Tuckett, Stacy O'Toole. Meredith Liu helped shape the ideas on how to publish it. Jeshurun Webb did amazing (and patient!) work designing it. Gretchen Eryl contributed her beautiful photography. The teachers from across America who share stories in this book, including Emily Lampe, Allison Kelly, Gabe Davis, Karen Kolman, Ray Schleck, Carolynn Molleur, David Collier, Meg Lafarge, and especially Ellie Brown, are most appreciated.

Fourth, all the folks who support Match Teacher Residency are wonderful, particularly Matt and Jenna Vettel, Bridgitt and Bruce Evans, Ann and Paul Sagan, Bob Manning and Yasmina Vinci, the New Schools Venture Fund, the Smith Family Foundation, the Carolyn and Peter Lynch Foundation, and most of all the Amelia Peabody Foundation.

Finally, to all the Match School parents in particular: you've taught us so much. We are grateful for the chance to work with your children. And we're always indebted to you for your support. We hope this book helps more teachers get to appreciate the joy of working collaboratively with parents — it's incredibly powerful and professionally satisfying.

Note:
Student names listed in the text have been changed. Some are names of students who applied to Match in our random lottery, but didn't get in, and so we've never even met them. Other names are our own biological children and loved ones.

Made in the USA
Middletown, DE
23 August 2017